A
# Pathway
Into
# The Holy Scripture
By

# William Tyndale

EDITED FOR

## 𝕿𝖍𝖊 𝕻𝖆𝖗𝖐𝖊𝖗 𝕾𝖔𝖈𝖎𝖊𝖙𝖞

BY THE
REV. HENRY WALTER, B.D. F.R.S

RECTOR OF HALISBURY BRYAN, DORSET;
FORMERLY FELLOW OF ST. JOHN'S COLLEGE, CAMBRIDGE, AND
PROFESSOR OF NATURAL PHILOSOPHY IN THE EAST INDIA
COMPANY'S COLLEGE AT HAILEYBURY

CAMBRIDGE:
PRINTED AT
THE UNIVERSITY PRESS
M.DCCC.L

*Hope. Inspiration. Trust.*

WE'RE SOCIAL! FOLLOW US FOR NEW TITLES AND DEALS:
FACEBOOK.COM/CROSSREACHPUBLICATIONS
@CROSSREACHPUB

**AVAILABLE IN PAPERBACK AND EBOOK EDITIONS**
PLEASE GO ONLINE FOR MORE GREAT TITLES
AVAILABLE THROUGH CROSSREACH PUBLICATIONS.
AND IF YOU ENJOYED THIS BOOK PLEASE CONSIDER LEAVING A
REVIEW ON AMAZON. THAT HELPS US OUT A LOT. THANKS.

© 2017 CROSSREACH PUBLICATIONS
ALL RIGHTS RESERVED, INCLUDING THE RIGHT TO REPRODUCE
THIS BOOK OR PORTIONS THEREOF IN ANY FORM WHATEVER.

# INTRODUCTORY NOTICE

[THE first original composition from Tyndale's pen, of which any trace or account has come down to us, is his 'Prologue' to the quarto edition of his translation of the New Testament. Indeed, the Rev. C. Anderson has not hesitated to say, that we have, in that Prologue, 'the very first language addressed by him to the Christians of England:' and if so, that first language is to be found in the 'Pathway into the Holy Scripture.' For the 'Pathway' is, in fact, a reprint of that Prologue; with such alterations as Tyndale either thought requisite to adapt it for separate publication, or expedient to prevent its identity with the reprobated Prologue from being detected at first sight. The precise date of the first publication of the Pathway, as a separate treatise, has not been ascertained. It is however mentioned by Dibdin, as having been printed by Thomas Godfray, London. Now the Prologue itself was undeniably printed in 1525, and Th. Godfray printed nothing after 1532; so that we have thus certain limits, between which the Pathway must have passed through the press. But farther, in Sir Thos. More's preface to his 'Confutation of Tyndale's Answer' to his Dialogue, which Confutation bears on its title-page that it was printed in 1532, we find him mentioning the Pathway, and apparently ignorant then that Tyndale was its author.

More had been recapitulating the titles of such works as had then come out in Tyndale's name, accompanying the recapitulation with brief but coarsely abusive comments, to prove him a 'setter-forth of heresies as evil as the Alchorane;' and then he proceeds to assail 'friar Barns, sometime doctor in Cambridge,' charging him with holding the heresy of Zuinglius 'concerning the sacrament of the altar,' (though Barnes's creed was in reality Lutheran,) for which, and for his demeanour, More says 'he might lawfully be burned,' as 'having clearly broken and forfeited the king's safe-conduct.' 'Then,' says he, 'have we farther yet, beside Barnes' book, the A. B. C. for children. And because there is no grace therein, lest we should lack prayers, we have the Prymer, and the Ploughman's Prayer, and a book of other small devotions, and then the whole Psalter too. After the Psalter, children were wont to go to their Donat and their Accydence; but now they go straight to scripture. And thereto have we, as a Donat, the book of *The Pathway to Scripture*; and for an Accydence, because we should be good scholars shortly and be soon sped, we have the whole Sum of Scripture in a little book: so that after these books well learned, we be meet for Tyndale's Pentateukes, and Tyndale's Testament, and all the other high heresies that he and Jaye, and Fryth, and friar Barns, teach in all their books beside; of all which heresies the seed is sown, and prettily sprung up in these little books before.'

The proclamations and episcopal mandates against the circulation of Tyndale's Testaments particularly notice the appended *glosses*; which belonged, exclusively, to the edition prefaced by that Prologue which was the prototype of the Pathway. And whilst that edition was well-nigh stifled in its birth by the anti-reforming zeal of Cochlæus, as noticed in the life of Tyndale, its prologue and pointed notes seem to have provoked the ruling powers at home to hunt it out for destruction with such successful zeal, that the fact of its ever having existed had begun to be overlooked, till a fragment of the portion printed at Cologne, probably lost by Tyndale in his hasty flight with the few finished sheets, was recently discovered in London, bound up with a contemporary production; and being purchased by the late Rt. Hon. Thomas Grenville, has just been added, by his considerate bequest, to the literary treasures of the British Museum. The account of this discovery, and the evidence for the genuineness of this fragment, which commences with the prologue, are stated by Mr Anderson as follows:—

"Mr Thomas Rodd, of Great Newport-street, a respectable bookseller in London, having exchanged with a friend, who did not recollect how he came by it, a quarto tract by Œcolampadius, without any cover, there was attached to it, by binding, a portion in the English language, black letter; and though it was evidently the gospel of Matthew, with *the prologge* of 14 pages preceding, neither Mr Rodd nor his friend understood, at the time, what it actually was. 'The accidental discovery,' says Mr R., 'of the remarkable initial letter Y, with which this page, the first of the prologue, is decorated, in another book printed at Cologne in 1534, first led me to search other books printed at the same place; and I succeeded in finding every cut and letter, with the exception of one, in other books from the same printing-office, that of Peter Quentel. I have found the type in which this portion of the New Testament is printed, and the cuts with which it is decorated, used in other books printed at Cologne from the year 1521 to 1540.' The fact is," proceeds Mr Anderson, "that though the tract entitled, *A Pathway into the Holy Scripture*, contains the most of it, the prologue was never printed entire in any subsequent edition, nor, above all, its important and beautiful introduction. Independently however of these proofs, there is incontrovertible evidence presented to the eye. The first page of the sacred text is preceded by a large, spirited cut of the evangelist Matthew at his work, dipping his pen into the inkstand, held out to him by an angel; and by this specimen, though the title-page be wanting, we are able to prove, not only that the printer was Peter Quentel, but that the year of printing was 1525. Rupert's commentary on Matthew, sent from Liege to Cologne, a closely-printed folio volume, was finished at Quentel's press so early as the 12th of June, 1526. Now as far back as the beginning of this folio, or page second, we have the identical large wood-cut of Matthew, which had been used to adorn the preceding New Testament; but, before being employed in the work of Rupert, better to fit the page, the block had been pared down, so as to deprive it of the pillar on the left side, the angel of the points of his pinions, and both pillars of their bases at the bottom. Thus also it was placed on the title-page, and again, next year, before Matthew, in a beautiful folio Latin Bible. In the New Testament of Tyndale, on the contrary, the block will be seen entire; consequently it must have been the prior publication, and must have been used accordingly in 1525."

By the kind indulgence of the late Mr Grenville, the editor was permitted to collate his unique copy of the Prologue. Such a collation was particularly desirable, because he has not been able to ascertain the existence of any copy of the Pathway, as separately printed; so that the only ancient edition of it, accessible to him, has been the copy inserted in Day's folio black-letter reprint of the works of Frith, Barnes, and Tyndale, published in 1573.

# A Pathway into the Holy Scriptures

Those portions of the Prologue which are omitted in the Pathway will be given to the reader in the notes appended to their proper places; and, on the other hand, such portions of the Pathway as were not parts of the Prologue will be distinguished, by including them within brackets. The marginal notes also, which appeared in the Prologue, and therefore passed under Tyndale's eye, will have the initials, W. T., affixed to them; whilst those that are only found in Day's edition will be marked Ant. ed., to express that they are not modern, and that yet it would not be just to hold Tyndale responsible for them, since they may have been no more than an editor's remarks, as it is obvious that some of the marginal notes in Day's volume must have been.]

# A PATHWAY

INTO

# THE HOLY SCRIPTURE

[I DO marvel greatly, dearly beloved in Christ, that ever any man should repugn or speak against the scripture to be had in every language, and that of every man. For I thought that no man had been] so blind to ask why light should be shewed to them that walk in darkness, where they cannot but stumble, and where to stumble is the danger of eternal damnation; other so despiteful that he would envy any man (I speak not his brother) so necessary a thing; or so Bedlam mad to affirm that good is the natural cause of evil, and darkness to proceed out of light, and that lying should be grounded in truth and verity; and not rather clean contrary, that light destroyeth darkness, and verity reproveth all manner lying.

[Nevertheless, seeing that it hath pleased God to send unto our Englishmen, even to as many as unfeignedly desire it, the scripture in their mother tongue, considering that there be in every place false teachers and blind leaders; that ye should be deceived of no man, I supposed it very necessary to prepare

# A Pathway into the Holy Scriptures

this Pathway into the scripture for you, that ye might walk surely, and ever know the true from the false: and, above all,] to put you in remembrance of certain points, which are, that ye well understand what these words mean; the Old Testament; the New Testament; the law; the gospel; Moses; Christ; nature; grace; working and believing; deeds and faith; lest we ascribe to the one that which belongeth to the other, and make of Christ Moses; of the gospel, the law; despise grace, and rob faith; and fall from meek learning into idle disputations; brawling and scolding about words.

The Old Testament is a book, wherein is written the law of God, and the deeds of them which fulfil them, and of them also which fulfil them not.

The New Testament is a book, wherein are contained the promises of God; and the deeds of them which believe them, or believe them not.

Evangelion (that we call the gospel) is a Greek word; and signifieth good, merry, glad and joyful tidings, that maketh a man's heart glad, and maketh him sing, dance, and leap for joy: as when David had killed Goliah the giant, came glad tidings unto the Jews, that their fearful and cruel enemy was slain, and they delivered out of all danger: for gladness whereof, they sung, danced, and were joyful. In like manner is the Evangelion of God (which we call gospel, and the New Testament) joyful tidings; and, as some say, a good hearing published by the apostles throughout all the world, of Christ the right David; how that he hath fought with sin, with death, and the devil, and overcome them: whereby all men that were in bondage to sin, wounded with death, overcome of the devil, are, without their own merits or deservings, loosed, justified, restored to life and saved, brought to liberty and reconciled unto the favour of God, and set at one with him again: which tidings as many as believe laud, praise, and thank God; are glad, sing and dance for joy.

This Evangelion or gospel (that is to say, such joyful tidings) is called the New Testament; because that as a man, when he shall die, appointeth his goods to be dealt and distributed after his death among them which he nameth to be his heirs; even so Christ before his death commanded and appointed that such Evangelion, gospel, or tidings should be declared throughout all the world, and therewith to give unto all that [repent, and] believe, all his goods: that is to say, his life, wherewith he swallowed and devoured up death; his righteousness, wherewith he banished sin; his salvation, wherewith he overcame eternal damnation. Now can the wretched man (that [knoweth himself to be wrapped] in sin, and in danger to death and hell) hear no more joyous a thing, than such glad and comfortable tidings of Christ; so that he cannot but be glad, and laugh from the low bottom of his heart, if he believe that the tidings are true.

To strength such faith withal, God promised this his Evangelion in the Old Testament by the prophets, as Paul saith, (Rom. 1), how that he was chosen out to preach God's Evangelion, which he before had promised by the prophets in the Scriptures, that treat of his Son which was born of the seed of David. In Gen. 3 God saith to the serpent, "I will put hatred between thee and the woman, between thy seed and her seed; that self seed shall tread thy head under foot." Christ is this woman's seed: he it is that hath trodden under foot the devil's head, that is to say, sin, death, hell, and all his power. For without this seed can no man avoid sin, death, hell, and everlasting damnation.

Again, (Gen. 22), God promised Abraham, saying, "In thy seed shall all the generations of the earth be blessed." Christ is that seed of Abraham, saith St Paul (Gal. 3). He hath blessed all the world through the gospel. For where Christ is not, there remaineth the curse, that fell on Adam as soon as he had sinned, so that they are in bondage under damnation of sin, death, and hell. Against this curse, blesseth now the gospel all the world inasmuch as it crieth openly, [unto all that knowledge their sins and repent, saying,] Whosoever believeth on the seed of Abraham shall be blessed; that is, he shall be delivered from sin, death, and hell, and shall henceforth continue righteous, and saved for ever; as Christ himself saith in the eleventh of John, 'He that believeth on me, shall never more die.'

"The law" (saith the gospel of John in the first chapter) "was given by Moses: but grace and verity by Jesus Christ." The law (whose minister is Moses) was given to bring us unto the knowledge of ourselves, that we might thereby feel and perceive what we are, of nature. The law condemneth us and all our deeds; and is called of Paul (in 2 Cor. 3) the ministration of death. For it killeth our consciences, and driveth us to desperation; inasmuch as it requireth of us that which is unpossible for our nature to do. It requireth of us the deeds of an whole man. It requireth perfect love, from the low bottom and ground of the heart, as well in all things which we suffer, as in the things which we do. But, saith John in the same place, "grace and verity is given us in Christ:" so that, when the law hath passed upon us, and condemned us to death (which is his nature to do), then we have in Christ grace, that is to say, favour, promises of life, of mercy, of pardon, freely, by the merits of Christ; and in Christ have we verity and truth, in that God [for his sake] fulfilleth all his promises to them that believe. Therefore is the Gospel the ministration of life. Paul calleth it, in the fore-rehearsed place of the 2 Cor. 3 the ministration of the Spirit and of righteousness. In the gospel, when we believe the promises, we receive the spirit of life; and are justified, in the blood of Christ, from all things whereof the law condemned us. [And we receive love unto the law, and power to fulfil it, and grow therein daily.] Of Christ it is written, in the fore-rehearsed John 1. This is he of whose abundance, or fulness, all we have received grace for grace, or favour for favour. That is to say, For the favour that God hath to his Son Christ, he giveth unto us his favour and good-will, [and all gifts of his grace,] as a father to his sons. As affirmeth Paul, saying, "Which loved us in his Beloved before the creation of the world." [So that Christ bringeth the love of God unto us, and not our own holy works.] Christ is made Lord over all, and is called in scripture God's mercy-stool: whosoever therefore flieth to Christ, can neither hear nor receive of God any other thing save mercy.

In the Old Testament are many promises, which are nothing else but the Evangelion or gospel, to save those that believed them from the vengeance of the law. And in the New Testament is oft made mention of the law, to condemn them which believe not the promises. Moreover, the law and the gospel may never be separate: for the gospel and promises serve but for troubled consciences, which are brought to desperation, and feel the pains of hell and death under the law, and are in captivity and bondage under the law. In all my deeds I must have the law before me, to condemn mine unperfectness. For all that I do (be I never so perfect) is yet damnable sin, when it is compared to the law, which requireth the ground and bottom of mine heart. I must therefore have always the law in my sight, that I may be meek in the spirit, and give God all the laud and praise, ascribing to him all righteousness, and to myself all unrighteousness and sin. I must also have the promises before mine eyes, that I despair not; in which promises I see the mercy, favour, and goodwill of God upon me in the blood of his Son Christ, which hath made satisfaction for mine unperfectness, and fulfilled for me that which I could not do.

Here may ye perceive that two manner of people are sore deceived. First, they which justify themselves with outward deeds, in that they abstain outwardly from that which the law forbiddeth, and do outwardly that which the law commandeth. They compare themselves to open sinners; and in respect of them justify themselves, condemning the open sinners. They set a vail on Moses' face, and see not how the law requireth love from the bottom of the heart, [and that love only is the fulfilling of the law.] If they did, they would not condemn their neighbours. "Love hideth the multitude of sins," saith St Peter in his first epistle. For whom I love from the deep bottom and ground of mine heart, him condemn I not, neither reckon his sins; but suffer his weakness and infirmity, as a mother the weakness of her son until he grow up into a perfect man.

Those also are deceived which, without all fear of God, give themselves unto all manner vices with full consent and full delectation, having no respect to the law of God (under whose vengeance they are locked up in captivity); but say, God is merciful, and Christ died for us; supposing that such dreaming and imagination is that faith which is so greatly commended in holy scripture. Nay, that is not faith, but rather a foolish blind opinion, springing of their own [corrupt] nature, and is not given them of the Spirit of God, [but rather of the spirit of the devil, whose faith now-a-days the popish compare and make equal unto the best trust, confidence, and belief, that a repenting soul can have in the blood of our Saviour Jesus, unto their own confusion, shame, and uttering what they are within. But] true faith is (as saith the apostle Paul) the gift of God; and is given to sinners, after the law hath passed upon them, and hath brought their consciences unto the brim of desperation and sorrows of hell.

They that have this right faith, consent to the law, that it is righteous and good; and justify God which made the law; and have delectation in the law (notwithstanding that they cannot fulfil it [as they would,] for their weakness); and they abhor whatsoever the law forbiddeth, though they cannot [always] avoid it. And their great sorrow is, because they cannot fulfil the will of God in the law; and the Spirit, that is in them, crieth to God night and day for strength and help, with tears (as saith Paul) that cannot be expressed with tongue. Of which things the belief of our popish (or of their) father, whom they so magnify for his strong faith, hath none experience at all.

The first, that is to say, he which justifieth himself with his outward deeds, consenteth not to the law inward, neither hath delectation therein, yea, he would rather that no such law were. So justifieth he not God, but hateth him as a tyrant; neither careth he for the promises, but will with his own strength be saviour of himself: no wise glorifieth he God, though he seem outward to do.

The second, that is to say, the sensual person, as a voluptuous swine, neither feareth God in his law, neither is thankful to him for his promises and mercy, which is set forth in Christ to all them that believe.

The right Christian man consenteth to the law that it is righteous, and justifieth God in the law; for he affirmeth that God is righteous and just, which is author of the law. He believeth the promises of God; and justifieth God, judging him true, and believing that he will fulfil his promises. With the law he condemneth himself, and all his deeds, and giveth all the praise to God. He believeth the promises, and ascribeth all truth to God: thus, everywhere, justifieth he God, and praiseth God.

By nature, through the fall of Adam, are we the children of wrath, heirs of the vengeance of God by birth, yea, and from our conception. And we have our fellowship with the damned devils, under the power of darkness and rule of Satan, while we are yet in our mother's wombs; and though we shew not forth the fruits of sin [as soon as we are born,] yet are we full of the natural poison, whereof all sinful deeds spring, and cannot but sin outwards, (be we never so young,) [as soon as we be able to work,] if occasion be given: for our nature is to do sin, as is the nature of a serpent to sting. And as a serpent, yet young, or yet unbrought forth, is full of poison, and cannot afterward (when the time is come, and occasion given) but bring forth the fruits thereof; and as an adder, a toad, or a snake, is hated of man, not for the evil that it hath done, but for the poison that is in it, and hurt which it cannot but do: so are we hated of God, for that natural poison, which is conceived and born with us, before we do any outward evil. And as the evil, which a venomous worm doth, maketh it not a serpent; but because it is a venomous worm, doth it evil and poisoneth: and as the fruit maketh not the tree evil; but because it is an evil tree, therefore bringeth it forth evil fruit, when the season of the fruit is: even so do not our evil deeds make us [first] evil, [though ignorance and blindness, through evil working, hardeneth us in evil, and maketh us worse and worse;] but because that of nature we are evil, therefore we both think and do evil, and are under vengeance under the law, convict to eternal damnation by the law, and are contrary to the will of God in all our will, and in all things consent to the will of the fiend.

By grace (that is to say, by favour) we are plucked out of Adam, the ground of all evil, and graffed in Christ, the root of all goodness. In Christ God loved us, his elect and chosen, before the world began, and reserved us unto the knowledge of his Son and of his holy gospel; and, when the gospel is preached to us, openeth our hearts, and giveth us grace to believe, and putteth the Spirit of Christ in us; and we know him as our Father most merciful, and consent to the law, and love it inwardly in our heart, and desire to fulfil it, and sorrow because we cannot: which will (sin we of frailty never so much) is sufficient, till more strength be given us; the blood of Christ hath made satisfaction for the rest; the blood of Christ hath obtained all things for us of God. Christ is our satisfaction, Redeemer, Deliverer, Saviour, from vengeance and wrath. Observe and mark in Paul's, Peter's and John's epistles, and in the gospel, what Christ is unto us.

# A Pathway into the Holy Scriptures

By faith are we saved only, in believing the promises. And though faith be never without love and good works, yet is our saving imputed neither to love nor unto good works, but unto faith only. For love and works are under the law, which requireth perfection and the ground and fountain of the heart, and damneth all imperfectness. Now is faith under the promises, which damn not; but give pardon, grace, mercy, favour, and whatsoever is contained in the promises.

Righteousness is divers: [for] blind reason imagineth many manner of righteousness. There is the righteousness of works (as I said before), when the heart is away, and feeleth not how the law is spiritual, and cannot be fulfilled, but from the bottom of the heart: as the just ministration of all manner of laws, and the observing of them, [for a worldly purpose and for our own profit, and not of love unto our neighbour, without all other respect,] and moral virtues, wherein philosophers put their felicity and blessedness, which all are nothing in the sight of God [in respect of the life to come.] There is in like manner the justifying of ceremonies, which some imagine their ownselves, some counterfeit other, saying in their blind reason, Such holy persons did thus and thus, and they were holy men; therefore if I do so likewise, I shall please God. But they have none answer of God, that that pleaseth. The Jews seek righteousness in their ceremonies, which God gave unto them, not for to justify, but to describe and paint Christ unto them: of which Jews testifieth Paul, saying, how that they have affection to God, but not after knowledge; for they go about to stablish their own justice, and are not obedient to the justice or righteousness that cometh of God, [which is the forgiveness of sin in Christ's blood unto all that repent and believe.] The cause is verily, that except a man cast away his own imagination and reason, he cannot perceive God, and understand the virtue and power of the blood of Christ. There is a full righteousness; when the law is fulfilled from the ground of the heart. This had neither Peter nor Paul in this life perfectly, [unto the uttermost, that they could not be perfecter,] but sighed after it. They were so far forth blessed in Christ, that they hungered and thirsted after it. Paul had this thirst; he consented to the law of God, that it ought so to be, but he found another lust in his members, contrary to the lust and desire of his mind, [that letted him,] and therefore cried out, saying, "O wretched man that I am! who shall deliver me from this body of death? thanks be to God through Jesus Christ." The righteousness that before God is of value, is to believe the promises of God, after the law hath confounded the conscience: as when the temporal law ofttimes condemneth the thief or murderer, and bringeth him to execution, so that he seeth nothing before him but present death; and then cometh good

# A Pathway into the Holy Scriptures

tidings, a charter from the king, and delivereth him. Likewise, when God's law hath brought the sinner into knowledge of himself, and hath confounded his conscience and opened unto him the wrath and vengeance of God; then cometh good tidings. The Evangelion sheweth unto him the promises of God in Christ, and how that Christ hath purchased pardon for him, hath satisfied the law for him, and appeased the wrath of God. And the poor sinner believeth, laudeth and thanketh God through Christ, and breaketh out into exceeding inward joy and gladness, for that he hath escaped so great wrath, so heavy vengeance, so fearful and so everlasting a death. And he henceforth is an hungred and athirst after more righteousness, that he might fulfil the law; and mourneth continually, commending his weakness unto God in the blood of our Saviour, Christ Jesus.

Here shall ye see compendiously and plainly set out the order and practice of every thing afore rehearsed.

The fall of Adam hath made us heirs of the vengeance and wrath of God, and heirs of eternal damnation; and hath brought us into captivity and bondage under the devil. And the devil is our lord, and our ruler, our head, our governor, our prince, yea, and our god. And our will is locked and knit faster unto the will of the devil, than could an hundred thousand chains bind a man unto a post.

## William Tyndale

Unto the devil's will consent we with all our hearts, with all our minds, with all our might, power, strength, will and lusts; [so that the law and will of the devil is written as well in our hearts as in our members, and we run headlong after the devil with full zeal, and the whole swing of all the power we have; as a stone cast up into the air cometh down naturally of his own self, with all the violence and swing of his own weight.] With what poison, deadly, and venomous hate hateth a man his enemy! With how great malice of mind, inwardly, do we slay and murder! With what violence and rage, yea, and with how fervent lust commit we advoutry, fornication, and such like uncleanness! With what pleasure and delectation, inwardly, serveth a glutton his belly! With what diligence deceive we! How busily seek we the things of this world! Whatsoever we do, think, or imagine, is abominable in the sight of God. [For we can refer nothing unto the honour of God; neither is his law, or will, written in our members or in our hearts: neither is there any more power in us to follow the will of God, than in a stone to ascend upward of his own self.] And [beside that,] we are as it were asleep in so deep blindness, that we can neither see nor feel what misery, thraldom, and wretchedness we are in, till Moses come and wake us, and publish the law. When we hear the law truly preached, how that we ought to love and honour God with all our strength and might, from the low

## A Pathway into the Holy Scriptures

bottom of the heart, [because he hath created us, and both heaven and earth for our sakes, and made us lord thereof;] and our neighbours (yea, our enemies) as ourselves, inwardly, from the ground of the heart, [because God hath made them after the likeness of his own image, and they are his sons as well as we, and Christ hath bought them with his blood, and made them heirs of everlasting life as well as us; and how we ought to] do whatsoever God biddeth, and abstain from whatsoever God forbiddeth, with all love and meekness, with a fervent and a burning lust from the center of the heart; then beginneth the conscience to rage against the law, and against God. No sea, be it ever so great a tempest, is so unquiet. For it is not possible for a natural man to consent to the law, that it should be good, or that God should be righteous which maketh the law; [inasmuch as it is contrary unto his nature, and damneth him and all that he can do, and neither sheweth him where to fetch help, nor preacheth any mercy; but only setteth man at variance with God, (as witnesseth Paul, Rom. 4) and provoketh him and stirreth him to rail on God, and to blaspheme him as a cruel tyrant. For it is not possible for a man, till he be born again, to think that God is righteous to make him of so poison a nature, either for his own pleasure or for the sin of another man, and to give him a law that is impossible for him to do, or to consent to;] his wit, reason, and will being so fast glued, yea, nailed and chained unto

*24*

the will of the devil. Neither can any creature loose the bonds, save the blood of Christ [only].

This is the captivity and bondage, whence Christ delivered us, redeemed and loosed us. His blood, his death, his patience in suffering rebukes and wrongs, his prayers and fastings, his meekness and fulfilling of the uttermost point of the law, appeased the wrath of God; brought the favour of God to us again; obtained that God should love us first, and be our Father, and that a merciful Father, that will consider our infirmities and weakness, and will give us his Spirit again (which was taken away in the fall of Adam) to rule, govern, and strength us, and to break the bonds of Satan, wherein we were so strait bound. When Christ is thuswise preached, and the promises rehearsed, which are contained in the prophets, in the psalms, and in divers places of the five books of Moses, [which preaching is called the Gospel or glad tidings;] then the hearts of them which are elect and chosen, begin to wax soft and melt at the bounteous mercy of God, and kindness shewed of Christ. For when the evangelion is preached, the Spirit of God entereth into them which God hath ordained and appointed unto eternal life; and openeth their inward eyes, and worketh such belief in them. When the woful consciences feel and taste how sweet a thing the bitter death of Christ is, and how merciful and loving God is, through Christ's purchasing and merits; they begin to love again, and to consent to the law of God, how that it is good and ought so to be, and that God is righteous which made it; and desire to fulfil the law, even as a sick man desireth to be whole, and are an hungred and thirst after more righteousness, and after more strength, to fulfil the law more perfectly. And in all that they do, or omit and leave undone, they seek God's honour and his will with meckness, ever condemning the unperfectness of their deeds by the law.

Now Christ standeth us in double stead; and us serveth, two manner wise. First, he is our Redeemer, Deliverer, Reconciler, Mediator, Intercessor, Advocate, Attorney, Solicitor, our Hope, Comfort, Shield, Protection, Defender, Strength, Health, Satisfaction and Salvation. His blood, his death, all that he ever did, is ours. And Christ himself, with all that he is or can do, is ours. His blood-shedding, and all that he did, doth me as good service as though I myself had done it. And God (as great as he is) is mine, with all that he hath, [as an husband is his wife's,] through Christ and his purchasing.

Secondarily, after that we be overcome with love and kindness, and now seek to do the will of God (which is a Christian man's nature), then have we Christ an example to counterfeit; as saith Christ himself in John, "I have given you an example." And in another evangelist he saith, "He that will be great among you, shall be your servant and minister; as the Son of man came to minister, and not to be ministered unto." And Paul saith, "Counterfeit Christ." And Peter saith, "Christ died for you, and left you an example to follow his steps." Whatsoever therefore faith hath received of God through Christ's blood and deserving, that same must love shed out, every whit, and bestow it on our neighbours unto their profit, yea, and that though they be our enemies. [What faith receiveth of God through Christ's blood, that we must bestow on our neighbours, though they be our enemies.] By faith we receive of God, and by love we shed out again. And that must we do freely, after the example of Christ, without any other respect, save our neighbour's wealth only; and neither look for reward in the earth, nor yet in heaven, for [the deserving and merits of] our deeds, [as friars preach; though we know that good deeds are rewarded, both in this life and in the life to come.] But of pure love must we bestow ourselves, all that we have, and all that we are able to do, even on our enemies, to bring them to God, considering nothing but their wealth, as Christ did ours. Christ did not his deeds to obtain heaven thereby, (that had been a madness;) heaven was his already, he was heir thereof, it was his by inheritance; but did them freely for our sakes, considering nothing but our wealth, and to bring the favour of God to us again, and us to God. And no natural son, that is his father's heir, doth his father's will because he would be heir; that he is already by

## A Pathway into the Holy Scriptures

birth; his father gave him that ere he was born, and is loather that he should go without it, than he himself hath wit to be; but of pure love doth he that he doth. And ask him, Why he doth any thing that he doth? he answereth, My father bade; it is my father's will; it pleaseth my father. Bond-servants work for hire, children for love: for their father, with all he hath, is theirs already. So doth a Christian man freely all that he doth; considereth nothing but the will of God, and his neighbour's wealth only. If I live chaste, I do it not to obtain heaven thereby; for then should I do wrong to the blood of Christ; Christ's blood hath obtained me that; Christ's merits have made me heir thereof; he is both door and way thitherwards: neither that I look for an higher room in heaven, than they shall have which live in wedlock, other than a whore of the stews (if she repent); for that were the pride of Lucifer: but freely to wait on the evangelion; [and to avoid the trouble of the world, and occasions that might pluck me therefrom,] and to serve my brother withal; even as one hand helpeth another, or one member another, because one feeleth another's grief, and the pain of the one is the pain of the other. Whatsoever is done to the least of us (whether it be good or bad), it is done to Christ; and whatsoever is done to my brother (if I be a Christian man), that same is done to me. Neither doth my brother's pain grieve me less than mine own: neither rejoice I less at his wealth than at mine own, [if I love him as well and as much as myself, as the law commandeth me.] If it were not so, how saith Paul? "Let him that rejoiceth, rejoice in the Lord," that is to say, Christ, which is Lord over all creatures. If my merits obtained me heaven, or a higher place there, then had I wherein I might rejoice besides the Lord.

Here see ye the nature of the law, and the nature of the evangelion; how the law is the key that bindeth and damneth all men, and the evangelion [is the key that] looseth them again. The law goeth before, and the evangelion followeth. When a preacher preacheth the law, he bindeth all consciences; and when he preacheth the gospel, he looseth them again. These two salves (I mean the law and the gospel) useth God and his preacher, to heal and cure sinners withal. The law driveth out the disease and maketh it appear, and is a sharp salve, and a fretting corosy, and killeth the dead flesh, and looseth and draweth the sores out by the roots, and all corruption. It pulleth from a man the trust and confidence that he hath in himself, and in his own works, merits, deservings and ceremonies, [and robbeth him of all his righteousness, and maketh him poor.] It killeth him, sendeth him down to hell, and bringeth him to utter desperation, and prepareth the way of the Lord, as it is written of John the Baptist. For it is not possible that Christ should come to a man, as long as he trusteth in himself, or in any worldly thing, [or hath any righteousness of his own, or riches of holy works.] Then cometh the evangelion, a more gentle plaster, which suppleth and suageth the wounds of the conscience, and bringeth health. It bringeth the Spirit of God; which looseth the bonds of Satan, and coupleth us to God and his will, through strong faith and fervent love, with bonds too strong for the devil, the world, or any creature to loose them. And the poor and wretched sinner feeleth so great mercy, love, and kindness in God, that he is sure in himself how that it is not possible that God should forsake him, or withdraw his mercy and love from him; and boldly crieth out with Paul, saying, "Who shall separate us from the love that God loveth us withal?" That is to say, What shall make me believe that God loveth me not? Shall tribulation? anguish? persecution? Shall hunger? nakedness? Shall sword? Nay, "I am sure that neither death, nor life, neither angel, neither rule nor power, neither present things nor things to come, neither high nor low, neither any creature, is able to separate us from the love of God, which is in Christ Jesu our Lord." In all such tribulations a Christian man perceiveth that God is his Father, and loveth him even as he loved Christ when he shed his blood on the cross. Finally, as before, when I was bond to the devil and his will, I wrought all manner evil and wickedness, not for hell's sake, which is the reward of sin, but because I was heir of hell by birth and

## WILLIAM TYNDALE

bondage to the devil, did I evil, (for I could none otherwise do; to do sin was my nature:) even so now, since I am coupled to God by Christ's blood, do I well, not for heaven's sake, [which is yet the reward of well doing;] but because I am heir of heaven by grace and Christ's purchasing, and have the Spirit of God, I do good freely, for so is my nature: as a good tree bringeth forth good fruit, and an evil tree evil fruit. By the fruits shall ye know what the tree is. A man's deeds declare what he is within, but make him neither good nor bad; [though, after we be created anew by the Spirit and doctrine of Christ, we wax perfecter alway, with working according to the doctrine, and not with blind works of our own imagining.] We must be first evil ere we do evil, as a serpent is first poisoned ere he poison. We must be also good ere we do good, as the fire must be first hot, ere it [heat another] thing. Take an example: As those blind and deaf, which are cured in the gospel, could not see nor hear, till Christ had given them sight and hearing; and those sick could not do the deeds of an whole man, till Christ had given them health; so can no man do good in his soul, till Christ have loosed him out of the bonds of Satan, and have given him wherewith to do good, yea, and first have poured into him that self good thing which he sheddeth forth afterward on other. Whatsoever is our own, is sin. Whatsoever is above that, is Christ's gift, purchase, doing and working. He bought it of his Father dearly, with his blood, yea, with his most bitter death, and gave his life for it. Whatsoever good thing is in us, that is given us freely, without our deserving or merits, for Christ's blood's sake. That we desire to follow the will of God, it is the gift of Christ's blood. That we now hate the devil's will (whereunto we were so fast locked, and could not but love it), is also the gift of Christ's blood; unto whom belongeth the praise and honour of our good deeds, and not unto us.

[Our deeds do us three manner of service. First, they certify us that we are heirs of everlasting life, and that the Spirit of God, which is the earnest thereof, is in us; in that our hearts consent unto the law of God, and we have power in our members to do it, though imperfectly. And secondarily, we tame the flesh therewith, and kill the sin that remaineth yet in us; and wax daily perfecter and perfecter in the Spirit therewith; and keep that the lusts choke not the word of God that is sown in us, nor quench the gifts and working of the Spirit, and that we lose not the Spirit again. And thirdly, we do our duty unto our neighbour therewith, and help their necessity unto our own comfort also, and draw all men unto the honouring and praising of God.

And whosoever excelleth in the gifts of grace, let the same think that they be given him, as much to do his brother service as for his own self, and as much for the love which God hath to the weak, as unto him unto whom God giveth such gifts. And he that withdraweth aught that he hath from his neighbour's need, robbeth his neighbour, and is a thief. And he that is proud of the gifts of God, and thinketh himself by the reason of them better than his feeble neighbour, and not rather (as the truth is) knowledgeth himself a servant unto his poor neighbour, by the reason of them; the same hath Lucifer's spirit in him, and not Christ's.

These things to know: first, the law; how that it is natural right, and equity; that we have but one God to put our hope and trust in, and him to love with all the heart, all the soul, and all our might and power, and neither to move heart nor hand but at his commandment, because he hath first created us of nought, and heaven and earth for our sakes; and afterwards when we had marred ourself through sin, he forgave us, and created us again, in the blood of his beloved Son:

And that we have the name of our one God in fear and reverence; and that we dishonour it not, in swearing thereby about light trifles or vanity, or call it to record for the confirming of wickedness or falsehood, or aught that is to the dishonour of God, which is the breaking of his laws, or unto the hurt of our neighbour:

# A Pathway into the Holy Scriptures

And inasmuch as he is our Lord and God, and we his double possession, by creation and redemption, and therefore ought (as I said) neither to move heart or hand without his commandment; it is right that we have needful holy days to come together, and learn his will, both the law which he will have us ruled by, and also the promises of mercy which he will have us trust unto; and to give God thanks together for his mercy, and to commit our infirmities to him through our Saviour Jesus, and to reconcile ourselves unto him, and each to other, if aught be between brother and brother that requireth it. And for this purpose and such like, as to visit the sick and needy, and redress peace and unity, were the holy days ordained only; and so far forth are they to be kept holy from all manner works that may be conveniently spared for the time, till this be done, and no further, but then lawfully to work:

And that it is right that we obey father and mother, master, lord, prince and king, and all the ordinances of the world, bodily and ghostly, by which God ruleth us, and ministereth freely his benefits unto us all: and that we love them for the benefits that we receive by them, and fear them for the power they have over us to punish us, if we trespass the law and good order. So far yet are the worldly powers or rulers to be obeyed only, as their commandments repugn not against the commandment of God; and then, ho. Wherefore we must have God's commandment ever in our hearts, and by the higher law interpret the inferior: that we obey nothing against the belief of one God, or against the faith, hope and trust that is in him only, or against the love of God, whereby we do or leave undone all things for his sake; and that we do nothing, for any man's commandment, against the reverence of the name of God, to make it despised, and the less feared and set by; and that we obey nothing to the hinderance of the knowledge of the blessed doctrine of God, whose servant the holy day is. Notwithstanding, though the rulers which God hath set over us command us against God, or do us open wrong, and oppress us with cruel tyranny; yet because they are in God's room, we may not avenge ourselves, but by the process and order of God's law, and laws of man made by the authority of God's law, which is also God's law, ever by an higher power, and remitting the vengeance unto God, and in the mean season suffer until the hour be come:

And on the other side, to know that a man ought to love his neighbour equally and fully as well as himself, because his neighbour (be he never so simple) is equally created of God, and as full redeemed by the blood of our Saviour Jesus Christ. Out of which commandment of love spring these: Kill not thy neighbour: defile not his wife: bear no false witness against him; and finally, not only do not these things in deed, but covet not in thine heart his house, his wife, his man-servant, maid-servant, ox, ass, or whatsoever is his: so that these laws, pertaining unto our neighbour, are not fulfilled in the sight of God, save with love. He that loveth not his neighbour keepeth not this commandment, 'Defile not thy neighbour's wife,' though he never touch her, or never see her, or think upon her. For the commandment is, Though thy neighbour's wife be never so fair, and thou have never so great opportunity given thee, and she consent, or haply provoke thee (as Potiphar's wife did Joseph), yet see thou love thy neighbour so well, that for very love thou cannot find in thine heart to do that wickedness. And even so he that trusteth in any thing, save in God only and in his Son Jesus Christ, keepeth no commandment at all, in the sight of God. For he that hath trust in any creature, whether in heaven or in earth, save in God and his Son Jesus, can see no cause to love God with all his heart, &c. neither to abstain from dishonouring his name, nor to keep the holy day for the love of his doctrine, nor to obey lovingly the rulers of this world; nor any cause to love his neighbour as himself, and to abstain from hurting him, where he may get profit by him, and save himself harmless. And in like wise, against this law, 'Love thy neighbour as thyself,' I may obey no worldly power, to do aught at any man's commandment unto the hurt of my neighbour that hath not deserved it, though he be a Turk:

And to know how contrary this law is unto our nature, and how it is damnation not to have this law written in our hearts, though we never commit the deeds; and how there is no other means to be saved from this damnation, than through repentance toward the law, and faith in Christ's blood; which are the very inward baptism of our souls, and the washing and the dipping of our bodies in the water is the outward sign. The plunging of the body under the water signifieth that we repent and profess to fight against sin and lusts, and to kill them every day more and more, with the help of God, and our diligence in following the doctrine of Christ and the leading of his Spirit; and that we believe to be washed from our natural damnation in which we are born, and from all the wrath of the law, and from all the infirmities and weaknesses that remain in us after we have given our consent unto the law, and yielded ourself to be scholars thereof; and from all the imperfectness of all our deeds done with cold love, and from all actual sin which shall chance on us, while we enforce the contrary and ever fight there against, and hope to sin no more. And thus repentance and faith begin at our baptism, and first professing the laws of God; and continue unto our lives' end, and grow as we grow in the Spirit: for the perfecter we be, the greater is our repentance, and the stronger our faith. And thus, as the Spirit and doctrine on God's part, and repentance and faith on our part, beget us anew in Christ, even so they make us grow, and wax perfect, and save us unto the end; and never leave us until all sin be put off, and we clean purified, and full formed, and fashioned after the similitude and likeness of the perfectness of our Saviour Jesus, whose gift all is:

And finally, to know that whatsoever good thing is in us, that same is the gift of grace, and therefore not of deserving, though many things be given of God through our diligence in working his laws, and chastising our bodies, and in praying for them, and believing his promises, which else should not be given us; yet our working deserveth not the gifts, no more than the diligence of a merchant in seeking a good ship bringeth the goods safe to land, though such diligence doth now and then help thereto: but when we believe in God, and then do all that is in our might, and not tempt him, then is God true to abide by his promise, and to help us, and perform alone when our strength is past:

These things, I say, to know, is to have all the scripture unlocked and opened before thee; so that if thou wilt go in, and read, thou canst not but understand. And in these things to be ignorant, is to have all the scripture locked up; so that the more thou readest it, the blinder thou art, and the more contrariety thou findest in it, and the more tangled art thou therein, and canst nowhere through: for if thou had a gloss in one place, in another it will not serve. And therefore, because we be never taught the profession of our baptism, we remain always unlearned, as well the spiritualty, for all their great clergy and high schools (as we say), as the lay people. And now, because the lay and unlearned people are taught these first principles of our profession, therefore they read the scripture, and understand and delight therein. And our great pillars of holy church, which have nailed a veil of false glosses on Moses's face, to corrupt the true understanding of his law, cannot come in. And therefore they bark, and say the scripture maketh heretics, and it is not possible for them to understand it in the English, because they themselves do not in Latin. And of pure malice, that they cannot have their will, they slay their brethren for their faith they have in our Saviour, and therewith utter their bloody wolfish tyranny, and what they be within, and whose disciples. Herewith, reader, be committed unto the grace of our Saviour Jesus; unto whom, and God our Father through him, be praise for ever and for ever. Amen.

# ABOUT CROSSREACH PUBLICATIONS

Thank you for choosing CrossReach Publications.

*Trust. Inspiration. Hope.*

These three words sum up the philosophy of why CrossReach Publications exist. We create trust with our customers by faithfully republishing yesterday's classics to create inspiration in the present thus inspiring hope for the future.

We are *non-denominational* and *non-sectarian.* We appreciate and respect what every part of the body brings to the table and believe everyone has the right to study and come to their own conclusions. We aim to help facilitate that end. Something for everyone. Occasionally we republish works outside of the Christian tradition in order to more fully facilitate learning and growth within the Church.

*We aspire to excellence.* If we have not met your standards please contact us and let us know. We want you to feel satisfied with your book. We publish quality books both in presentation and content from a wide variety of authors who span various doctrinal positions and traditions, on a wide variety of Christian topics that will teach, encourage, challenge, inspire and equip.

*We're a family-based home-business.* A husband and wife team raising 8 kids. If you have any questions or comments about our publications contact us:

ContactUs@CrossReach.net
YouTube.com/c/TheKinsellaBunchVlog

Don't forget you can follow us on Facebook and Twitter, (addresses are on the copyright page above) to keep up to date on our newest titles and deals.

# BESTSELLING TITLES FROM CROSSREACH[1]

God Still Speaks
A. W. Tozer
€6.99
https://amazon.com/dp/154980894X

Tozer is as popular today as when he was living on the earth. He is respected right across the spectrum of Christianity, in circles that would disagree sharply with him doctrinally. Why is this? A. W. Tozer was a man who knew the voice of God. He shared this experience with every true child of God. With all those who are called by the grace of God to share in the mystical union that is possible with Him through His Son Jesus.

Tozer fought against much dryness and formality in his day. Considered a mighty man of God by most Evangelicals today, he was unconventional in his approach to spirituality and had no qualms about consulting everyone from Catholic Saints to German Protestant mystics for inspiration on how to experience God more fully.

Tozer, just like his Master, doesn't fit neatly into our theological boxes. He was a man after God's own heart and was willing to break the rules (man-made ones that is) to get there.

---

[1] Most of our eBooks cost between $0.99 and $1.99. Most of our paperbacks cost $7.99 or less. Click on the title of each to be brought to the eBook edition or if this is a paperback, then copy the address into your internet browser. Buy from CrossReach Publications for quality and price. We have a full selection of titles in print and eBook, available on Amazon and a growing selection other online stores. You can see our full selection just by searching for CrossReach Publications in the search bar!

Here are two writings by Tozer that touch on the heart of this goal. Revelation is Not Enough and The Speaking Voice. A bonus chapter The Menace of the Religious Movie is included.

This is meat to sink your spiritual teeth into. Tozer's writings will show you the way to satisfy your spiritual hunger.

How to Be Filled with the Holy Spirit
A. W. Tozer
$6.99
https:// amazon.com/dp/1549774190

Before we deal with the question of how to be filled with the Holy Spirit, there are some matters which first have to be settled. As believers you have to get them out of the way, and right here is where the difficulty arises. I have been afraid that my listeners might have gotten the idea somewhere that I had a how-to-be-filled-with-the-Spirit-in-five-easy-lessons doctrine, which I could give you. If you can have any such vague ideas as that, I can only stand before you and say, "I am sorry"; because it isn't true; I can't give you such a course. There are some things, I say, that you have to get out of the way, settled.

The 400 Silent Years
H. A. Ironside
$7.50
https://amazon.com/dp/1549816039

Fully illustrated. Includes all of the drawings from the original edition.
What is the history between the Old and New Testaments? Most people are not even aware there is such a gap. But there is. A 400 year gap.

When the Old Testament leaves off the Jews have just returned back from Babylonian captivity and the Persian Empire is in full swing. When Jesus enters the scene it is 400 years later. The Persians are long gone, the Greeks have had their time and now the Romans rule to roost.

So what happened? Do we have any writings from this time? Could understanding this period of time help us understand the New Testament, the world of Jesus and the Apostles? The answer is yes.

This exciting book by well-known author H. A. Ironside lifts the veil from this vital period of Jewish history and helps piece together the events that brought them from Malachi to Matthew.

This book will be of interested to students of Biblical, Ancient Near Eastern, Greek and Roman history as well as all those who desire to know and understand the Bible for fully.

Christianity and Liberalism
J. Gresham Machen

The purpose of this book is not to decide the religious issue of the present day, but merely to present the issue as sharply and clearly as possible, in order that the reader may be aided in deciding it for himself. Presenting an issue sharply is indeed by no means a popular business at the present time; there are many who prefer to fight their intellectual battles in what Dr. Francis L. Patton has aptly called a "condition of low visibility." Clear-cut definition of terms in religious matters, bold facing of the logical implications of religious views, is by many persons regarded as an impious proceeding. May it not discourage contribution to mission boards? May it not hinder the progress of consolidation, and produce a poor showing in columns of Church statistics? But with such persons we cannot possibly bring ourselves to agree. Light may seem at times to be an impertinent intruder, but it is always beneficial in the end. The type of religion which rejoices in the pious sound of traditional phrases, regardless of their meanings, or shrinks from "controversial" matters, will never stand amid the shocks of life. In the sphere of religion, as in other spheres, the things about which men are agreed are apt to be the things that are least worth holding; the really important things are the things about which men will fight.

The Two Babylons
Alexander Hislop
$7.99
https://amazon.com/dp/1549771191

Fully Illustrated High Res. Images. Complete and Unabridged.
Expanded Seventh Edition. This is the first and only seventh edition available in a modern digital edition. Nothing is left out! New material not found in the first six editions!!! Available in eBook and paperback edition exclusively from CrossReach Publications.

"In his work on "The Two Babylons" Dr. Hislop has proven conclusively that all the idolatrous systems of the nations had their origin in what was founded by that mighty Rebel, the beginning of whose kingdom was Babel (Gen. 10:10)."—A. W. Pink, The Antichrist (1923)

There is this great difference between the works of men and the works of God, that the same minute and searching investigation, which displays the defects and imperfections of the one, brings out also the beauties of the other. If the most finely polished needle on which the art of man has been expended be subjected to a microscope, many inequalities, much roughness and clumsiness, will be seen. But if the microscope be brought to bear on the flowers of the field, no such result appears. Instead of their beauty diminishing, new beauties and still more delicate, that have escaped the naked eye, are forthwith discovered; beauties that make us appreciate, in a way which otherwise we could have had little conception of, the full force of the Lord's saying, "Consider the lilies of the field, how they grow; they toil not, neither do they spin: and yet I say unto you, That even Solomon, in all his glory, was not arrayed like one of these." The same law appears also in comparing the Word of God and the most finished productions of men. There are spots and blemishes in the most admired productions of human genius. But the more the Scriptures are searched, the more minutely they are studied, the more their perfection appears; new beauties are brought into light every day; and the discoveries of science, the researches of the learned, and the labours of infidels, all alike conspire to illustrate the wonderful harmony of all the parts, and the Divine beauty that clothes the whole. If this be the case with Scripture in general, it is especially the case with prophetic Scripture. As every spoke in the wheel of Providence revolves, the prophetic symbols start into still more bold and beautiful relief. This is very strikingly the case with the prophetic language that forms the groundwork and cornerstone of the present work. There never has been any difficulty in the mind of any enlightened Protestant in identifying the woman "sitting on seven mountains," and having on her forehead the name written, "Mystery, Babylon the Great," with the Roman apostacy.

What We Are In Christ
E. W. Kenyon
$5.99
https://amazon.com/dp/1549823094

I was surprised to find that the expressions "in Christ," "in whom," and "in Him" occur more than 130 times in the New Testament. This is the heart of the Revelation of Redemption given to Paul. Here is the secret of faith—faith that conquers, faith that moves mountains. Here is the secret of the Spirit's guiding us into all reality. The heart craves intimacy with the Lord Jesus and with the Father. This craving can now be satisfied.

Ephesians 1:7: "In whom we have our redemption through his blood, the remission of our trespasses according to the riches of his grace."

It is not a beggarly Redemption, but a real liberty in Christ that we have now. It is a Redemption by the God Who could say, "Let there be lights in the firmament of heaven," and cause the whole starry heavens to leap into being in a single instant. It is Omnipotence beyond human reason. This is where philosophy has never left a footprint.

The Complete Wycliffe Bible: Old Testament, New Testament & Apocrypha: Text Edition
$18.99
https:// amazon.com/dp/154978692X

In making this edition of Wycliffe's monumental work the Publisher has had to make a number of decisions that affect the final outcome of the work. Some of these decisions may be welcomed by the reading public and some perhaps not. All of the decisions were made with the reader in mind. Our intention was to produce an edition of Wycliffe's Bible translation that was reasonably priced and to do this it must be in one volume. This has meant choosing a large paper format. Other smaller sized editions are over 800 pages. We chose a larger paper size that results in around 250 pages less. We chose a font that is recognized as easily readable at smaller sizes. Adobe Garamond, 10 pt. was selected. We have tested it and have not found it to be an uncomfortable reading size. If you have reasonable eyesight, you will not need a magnifying glass, as has been reportedly needed for other modern reprints. We hope you like it. Some will complain that we have not inserted indents and paragraphing. Again, this is a massive volume and we have tried to produce a book that is within one volume so that it is commercially viable for us and you the reader. It has also meant not including any of the introductions by Wycliffe, Jerome and others, or notes that were a part of the original. Hence the subtitle "Text Edition". We understand this will not be to everyone's liking, but we are limited, by the printer, to how many pages our books can be. At the size we chose we are almost at capacity. At a smaller size we could have done over 800 pages, but we still would have had to cram the same amount of text in. So the problem would be the same. The only way around this problem would have been to produce two large volumes and at this time we do question the viability of such an undertaking. However, if it is clear that there is a great demand for it, we may bring out a new two volume edition with that additional text. This work was first produced in the late Middle Ages. The language is therefore extremely archaic. So much so that some of the letters have evolved and changed since then. This edition contains all modern letters, but does not contain modern spelling. It is therefore, not a "Modern Edition" in this sense. The yogh for example has been replaced as necessary. Purists will complain, but we hope for the average reader this will not present much of a problem. It will hopefully give the reader a text as close to the original yet still possible to be read and, with a little work, understood.

How to Prepare Sermons
William Evans
$7.99
https://amazon.com/dp/154981785X

This volume is not an attempt to present a complete and exhaustive treatment on Homiletics—the science and art of preaching, for there are already on the market larger and more comprehensive works on the subject. This book is prepared not only for theological students but also to supply the need of such as find themselves denied the privileges of a regular ministerial training, but who, nevertheless, feel themselves called upon to preach or proclaim the gospel of the Lord Jesus Christ. Indeed the lectures herein printed are in substance the same as delivered to young men and women preparing themselves for Christian service in a Bible training school. This fact accounts for their conversational style, which the author has not deemed wise to change. Christian laymen, even though not preachers in the accepted sense of that term, desiring to be able to prepare brief gospel addresses and Bible readings, will find the help they need in this volume. Those seeking help in the preparation of "talks" for young peoples' societies, conventions, leagues, etc., may receive hints and suggestions in this work. The book contains theory and practice. Part One deals with the method of constructing various kinds of sermons and Bible addresses. Part Two is composed of outlines illustrating Part One. The closing chapter on "Illustrations and Their Use" has been found so helpful wherever delivered that it is thought advisable to give it a place in this volume.

A Medicine Chest for Christian Practitioners
Clarence Larkin
$4.99
https://amazon.com/dp/1520411316

This booklet is designed to give tools for Christian service. Clarence Larkin was born October 28, 1850, in Chester, Delaware County, Pennsylvania. He was converted to Christ at the age of 19. He was a mechanical engineer, teacher and manufacturer by trade. In 1884, at the age of 34, he became an ordained Baptist minister. His first pastorate was at Kennett Square, Pennsylvania; his second was at Fox Chase, Pennsylvania, where he remained for 20 years. He was not a premillennialist at the time of his ordination, but his study of the Scriptures, with the help of some books that fell into his hands, led him to adopt the premillennialist position. He began to make large wall charts, which he titled, "Prophetic Truth," for use in the pulpit. These led to his being invited to teach, in connection with his pastoral work, in two Bible institutes. During this time he published a number of prophetical charts, which were widely circulated. He spent three years of his life designing and drawing the charts and preparing the text for his most noteworthy book "Dispensational Truth." Because it had a large and wide circulation in this and other lands, the first edition was soon exhausted. It was followed by a second edition, and then, realizing that the book was of permanent value, Larkin revised it and expanded it, printing it in its present form. Larkin followed this masterpiece with other books. During the last five years of his life, the demand for Larkin's books made it necessary for him to give up the pastorate and devote his full time to writing. He went to be with the Lord on January 24, 1924.—The Christian Worker's Outfit

Claiming Our Rights
E. W. Kenyon
$7.99
www.amazon.com/dp/1549815148

There is no excuse for the spiritual weakness and poverty of the Family of God when the wealth of Grace and Love of our great Father with His power and wisdom are all at our disposal. We are not coming to the Father as a tramp coming to the door begging for food; we come as sons not only claiming our legal rights but claiming the natural rights of a child that is begotten in love. No one can hinder us or question our right of approach to our Father.

Satan has Legal Rights over the sinner that God cannot dispute or challenge. He can sell them as slaves; he owns them, body, soul and spirit. But the moment we are born again... receive Eternal Life, the nature of God,—his legal dominion ends.

Christ is the Legal Head of the New Creation, or Family of God, and all the Authority that was given Him, He has given us: (Matthew 28:18), "All authority in heaven," the seat of authority, and "on earth," the place of execution of authority.

He is "head over all things," the highest authority in the Universe, for the benefit of the Church which is His body.

The Person and Work of the Holy Spirit
R. A. Torey
$5.85
www.amazon.com/dp/1549821490

Before one can correctly understand the work of the Holy Spirit, he must first of all know the Spirit Himself. A frequent source of error and fanaticism about the work of the Holy Spirit is the attempt to study and understand His work without first of all coming to know Him as a Person.
It is of the highest importance from the standpoint of worship that we decide whether the Holy Spirit is a Divine Person, worthy to receive our adoration, our faith, our love, and our entire surrender to Himself, or whether it is simply an influence emanating from God or a power or an illumination that God imparts to us. If the Holy Spirit is a person, and a Divine Person, and we do not know Him as such, then we are robbing a Divine Being of the worship and the faith and the love and the surrender to Himself which are His due.

Home Geography for the Primary Grades
C. C. Long
$7.95
https://amazon.com/dp/1518780660

A popular homeschooling resource for many generations now. Geography may be divided into the geography of the home and the geography of the world at large. A knowledge of the home must be obtained by direct observation; of the rest of the world, through the imagination assisted by information. Ideas acquired by direct observation form a basis for imagining those things which are distant and unknown. The first work, then, in geographical instruction, is to study that small part of the earth's surface lying just at our doors. All around are illustrations of lake and river, upland and lowland, slope and valley. These forms must be actually observed by the pupil, mental pictures obtained, in order that he may be enabled to build up in his mind other mental pictures of similar unseen forms. The hill that he climbs each day may, by an appeal to his imagination, represent to him the lofty Andes or the Alps. From the meadow, or the bit of level land near the door, may be developed a notion of plain and prairie. The little stream that flows past the schoolhouse door, or even one formed by the sudden shower, may speak to him of the Mississippi, the Amazon, or the Rhine. Similarly, the idea of sea or ocean may be deduced from that of pond or lake. Thus, after the pupil has acquired elementary ideas by actual perception, the imagination can use them in constructing, on a larger scale, mental pictures of similar objects outside the bounds of his own experience and observation.

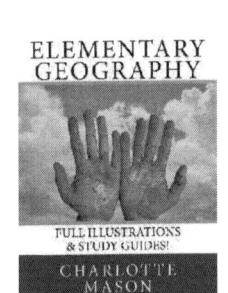

<u>Elementary Geography</u>
Charlotte Mason
$8.99
https://amazon.com/dp/1549774859

This little book is confined to very simple "reading lessons upon the Form and Motions of the Earth, the Points of the Compass, the Meaning of a Map: Definitions."

It is hoped that these reading lessons may afford intelligent teaching, even in the hands of a young teacher.

Children should go through the book twice, and should, after the second reading, be able to answer any of the questions from memory.

WE OFFER A LARGE & GROWING SELECTION OF CHRISTIAN TITLES
ALL AVAILABLE THROUGH AMAZON & OTHER ONLINE STORES
JUST SEARCH FOR CROSSREACH PUBLICATIONS!

Made in the USA
Middletown, DE
22 February 2021

34202115R00031